Modern Sicily: The History and Legacy of the Mediterra[n] Middle Ages

By Charles River Editors

Franz Clemens' picture of the ruins of a temple at Solunto

About Charles River Editors

Charles River Editors is a boutique digital publishing company, specializing in bringing history back to life with educational and engaging books on a wide range of topics. Keep up to date with our new and free offerings with this 5 second sign up on our weekly mailing list, and visit Our Kindle Author Page to see other recently published Kindle titles.

We make these books for you and always want to know our readers' opinions, so we encourage you to leave reviews and look forward to publishing new and exciting titles each week.

Introduction

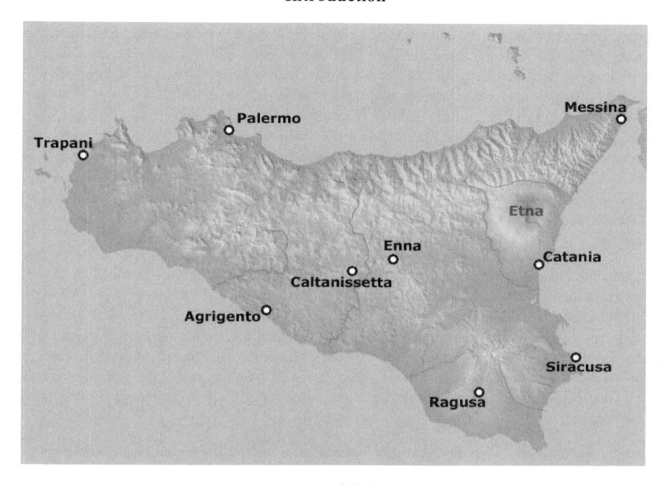

A map of Sicily

Sicily

It is hard to find an island on the map more central than Sicily. Located at the crossroads between Europe and Africa, and between the Eastern and Western Mediterranean, Sicily has rarely been governed as an independent, unified state. Nonetheless, the island has always occupied a front-row seat to some of the most important events in history, and nowhere is this more obvious than during antiquity.

Very fertile in ancient times, Sicily was especially prized for its grain production. The island had been inhabited by native tribes since prehistoric times, but by the 9th and 8th centuries BCE, Sicily would be the staging area for a confrontation between the Greeks and the Phoenicians, seafaring powers that scrambled to establish colonies along its coasts. These colonies, in time, would grow independent, and by the Classical era (510-323 BCE), they would be waging wars of their own.

It was during the Classical era that, especially under the tyrants (dictators) of the Greek city of Syracuse, Sicily came the closest to being governed as a single, unified, and independent state. In time, it came to challenge the powerful trade empire of Carthage, a former Phoenician colony in North Africa, and it vied with the cities and kingdoms of mainland Greece for primacy in the Greek world. Later on, Sicily would be both a prize and a battlefield during the First Punic War (263-241 BCE) and, to a lesser degree, also during the Second Punic War (218-201 BCE). These were massive, protracted conflicts between Carthage and the rising Roman Republic, and Rome would subsequently become the main power in the Mediterranean on its way to ruling much of the known world. Sicily would go on to become the Roman Republic's first territory outside of Italy and its first province; and Hieron, the tyrant of Syracuse at the time, would be Rome's first client king. Thus, the two different models through which Rome would control its empire in the future made their first appearance in Sicily. The province of Sicily would furthermore be crucial when it came to providing funds, and especially grain, to the rising Roman Republic.

After the Punic Wars, Sicily would remain a Roman domain until the end of antiquity, and affairs on the island dramatically affected the Romans at home. The First Servile War (135-132 BCE) and Second Servile War (104-100 BCE) both took place in Sicily, and they were perhaps the largest (and temporarily successful) slave revolts in antiquity, demonstrating a great unease in the early stages of Roman imperialism. In 70 BCE, the Roman orator and statesman Cicero gave a speech against Verres, the corrupt governor of the island, and over 2,000 years later it still provides an invaluable glimpse into the way things were run in Sicily and the Roman Republic as a whole.

Although the conquest of Egypt in 30 BCE would strip Sicily of its central role as Rome's main supplier of grain, the island would remain an important part of the Roman Empire for about 500 more years. Sicily would only become independent again after the fall of the Western Roman Empire to barbarian tribes in the late 5th century CE, which ushered in the beginning of the Middle Ages.

Over 1500 years later, the largest island of the Mediterranean remains a complicated place with a fraught relationship to the Italian mainland. Separated by only the narrow Strait of Messina, Sicily feels like a different country in many ways, and the differences between Sicilians and Italians are much vaster than the tiny geographical separating them might intimate. For example, the linguistic differences between the two are substantial, as Sicilian is practically its own language, rather than just a dialect. It differs from Italian most apparently insofar as the normal final "o" of masculine nouns is replaced by a "u," but beyond that difference, there are lengthy, five syllable words that a standard Italian tongue tends to trip over. In fact, most Italians have difficulty understanding Sicilian if they can comprehend any of it at all.

There is also an ethnic difference between Sicilians and Italians. Most notably, many Sicilians have bright red hair and light eyes, which is usually thought to be a result of the Norman invasions, although today some historians believe it is because of the strong presence of the British during the Napoleonic Wars, as well as the Anglo-American occupation of Italy during World War II. Even Sicilian cuisine varies from the Italian mainland - Sicily is celebrated for having 72 different kinds of bread, and Sicilians often eat ice cream (gelato) for breakfast.

However diverse Sicily might be, it is also paradoxically considered to be an emblem of Italy itself, a paradox it shares with Naples. No writer put it more aptly than the great Romantic poet Goethe. In an April 13, 1787 letter from Palermo, published in Journey to Italy, Goethe made the following declaration: "To have seen Italy without having seen Sicily is not to have seen Italy at all, for Sicily is the clue to everything." As Goethe's words suggest, Sicily is unquestionably unique thanks to its turbulent and rich history, but it shares the same qualities as the Italian nation overall, from its beautiful scenery, delicious cuisine, dazzling sunshine, and unparalleled cultural production to its problems with law and order, and its seeming impenetrability to outside visitors. Through it all, Sicily has been a true cultural melting pot, one that is responsible for some of the greatest contributions to Western culture.

Modern Sicily: The History and Legacy of the Mediterranean Island Since the Middle Ages looks at one of the world's most important and contested territories. Along with pictures depicting important people, places, and events, you will learn about Sicily like never before.

A Description of Sicily

The 19th century writer E.A. Freeman described Sicily as "the central island of the civilized world" (Freeman 1891: 49). While this description is dated, it emphasized the importance of Sicily's position, located at the center of the Mediterranean Sea between Italy and Africa. It controls the pass between the Eastern and Western Mediterranean by sea, the pass between Italy and Europe to the north, and Tunis and Africa to the south by land. Sicily is furthermore the largest island in the Mediterranean. Its shape is practically like a triangle, with angles pointing west, northeast and southeast, and the tip of its western point slightly cut off. To the northeast, Sicily is located so close to Italy (the crossing between the tip of Italy's "boot" and the northeastern point of Sicily at its narrowest is less than two miles wide) that it was believed in ancient times to have once formed a contiguous landmass with the mainland (Freeman: 51-54; Polybius, *Histories*, I, 42).

A map highlighting the location of Sicily

In antiquity, the island of Sicily was very fertile and suited for agriculture. It was rich in wine, and, especially, in grain. Thus, it should come as little surprise that the worship of Demeter, the goddess of agriculture, was widespread on the island. Sicily was also famously rich, both in mythological and in historic times, in livestock, with many sheep and cattle (tangentially, it was one of the birthplaces of bucolic poetry in the 4th century BCE) and fast horses. Several Olympic victories for Sicilians are recorded, especially in chariot-racing and horse-racing events (Freeman: 91-96).

Despite its fertility, however, the island as a whole is also very mountainous. There was always a strong a division between the coasts and the interior of the island: in the Classical period, colonists like the Greeks and Phoenicians tended to keep to the coasts, while the interior of the island was inhabited by more or less independent native states for a very long time (Freeman: 54-56). In later times, armies wishing to avoid capture or confrontation would pass through the interior of the island, and revolts would almost invariably make their headquarters in one of the inland cities.

On the northeastern corner of Sicily lies the city of Messene, or Messana in the Dorian dialect of Greek, opposite of the mainland Italian city of Rhegium. Another important city along the north coast of the island was Panormus (Freeman: 57-61). On Sicily's western tip, Eryx and Lilybaeum share the two points left by the cut-off third angle of the Sicilian "triangle", along with small the island (once a peninsula) of Motya (Freeman: 61-62). Along or near the south coast we find the cities of Selinus, Acragas, Gela and Morgantina (Freeman: 62-64). However, although many of these cities were important in their own right, it is the eastern coast of the island which was the focal point for much of Sicily's ancient history, as it was the location of the most and the most important Greek colonies. Near Sicily's southeastern corner lies the town of Syracuse, which would prove to be the most significant Greek city of the island in ancient times. Important geographic features of Syracuse include its impressive harbor, and the nearby island of Ortygia, which the Syracusans fortified and artificially turned into a peninsula (the ancient poet Ibycus even wrote a poem about the feat: see Ibycus, fr. 321). North of Syracuse we find the cities of Hyblaean Megara, Camarina, Leontini, Catana and Tauromenium (Freeman: 65-67). Among the inland towns, often fenced off by the island's large mountain ranges, including most impressively Eryx and the volcano Aetna, we find most importantly Henna and Centurippa (Freeman: 67-71). The volcanic nature of the island also leads to such interesting geological features as mud volcanoes and hot springs. The island also possesses large limestone quarries and is surrounded by a number of smaller islands and groups of islands, such as Lipara and the Aeolian islands, the Aegates and Aegousa. However, the most important of these islands, Malta, was in ancient times much more closely linked to Africa than to Europe or Sicily.

To refer to Sicily is actually to refer to a fair number of other small islands that surround it at various distances, all of which were formed thousands of years ago by the volcanic activity beneath the surface of the sea. To give a brief orientation, off the western coast is the Aegadian group of islands, that includes Favignana of the famous mattanza (tuna hunting) tradition. These islands were the site of the Romans' decisive victory over Carthage in the First Punic War. Off the northern coast are the seven Aeolian Islands, including Lipari, the largest island and currently a major tourism hub. They are volcanic in origin and form a subterranean link between the major volcanoes of Etna (on Sicily) and Vesuvius (near Naples). One of the seven Aeolian Islands, Stromboli is still regularly active; it spews streams of lava on its small population to the delight of the tourists who regularly trek up its fertile slopes. In addition to being famous for their intense winds that actually can cut off the two most distant islands from the outside world, these islands produce Sicily's famous green salty caper berries and are also rich in pumice stone. To the north west of Sicily is the island of Ustica, an ancient settlement and rocky island that served as a penal colony until the 1950s. The island of Pantelleria, also a former penal settlement, is found south west of Sicily; its volcanic origins have made it a famous destination for hot mineral springs. Inhabited since early antiquity, Pantelleria was home to Neolithic settlers who constructed ramparts and tombs with the blocks of lava readily at their disposal. Most prominent in recent news is the island of Lampedusa which is found south west of Sicily, and which was likely given its name (rocky in Greek) because of its rugged terrain. The southernmost part of Italy, it is closer to Tunisia at 70 miles away than to Sicily at 127 miles away. Due to its proximity to Africa, it is a frequent landing point for refugees fleeing Libya.

Ben Aveling's picture of Mount Etna

The ancient myths and the pagan deities worshipped in Sicily, both native and Greek - the various myths often influenced each other, and there may even have been Phoenician/Carthaginian elements in some of the cults - were not unrelated to the island's geography. According to ancient mythology, the fire-breathing giant Enceladus, who had attempted to overthrow the gods, was buried under the island, which had been hurled at him by Zeus or Athena. This giant caused earthquakes, and he was said to be the cause of the fire erupting from the volcanic Mount Etna. Throughout the island, there were also locations sacred to Hephaestus, the god of fire and metalwork. And the goddess of grain, Demeter, who was naturally widely worshipped on the fertile island, was linked to the underworld by the legend of the abduction of her daughter Persephone by Hades, the king of the underworld. Other deities worshipped in Sicily included various river and spring gods, and according to legend, Sicily was also the location for some of the hero Odysseus's adventures in the *Odyssey*. Sicily was the home of the Laestrygonians (Homer, *The Odyssey,* X, 80-132), the monsters Scylla and Charybdis in the straits between Sicily and Italy (Odyssey, XII, 234-260), and the one-eyed giants called the Cyclopes (*Odyssey,* IX, 105-566), who also feature in other myths, such as that of Acis and Galatea (Ovid, *Metamorphoses*, XIII, 738-788) (Freeman: 71-91).

Ben Aveling's picture of Mount Etna

Today, Sicily has a population of around five million people in total, compared to the 60 million inhabitants of Italy; remarkably, its population has only grown about five times the size it was during the Roman Empire. This relatively small population growth is attributable to the fact that a large part of the inner island is inhospitable. This topographical limitation was never overcome, no doubt thanks to the years of harsh rule from various foreign invaders who thought more of their own interests than the consistent development of the Sicilian economy. Thus, Sicilians emigrated in large numbers, contributing to a vast global diaspora that left the population of Sicilians living on the island relatively small in comparison.

Sicily's Early History

Prehistoric Sicily is relatively well documented, thanks to a rich trove of archeological evidence that has been unearthed over the course of its entire history, giving historians and archeologists a better picture of what life was like ten thousand years ago. Most remarkably, in pre-Socratic times, the philosopher Xenophanes was already speculating about the island's past, as he observed fish and seaweed fossils in the quarries near Syracuse. Then, new interest was sparked in the Renaissance that continued through to the eighteenth century. The result of all this attention to the antiquities of Sicily is that archeologists are able to assert that between 8000 and 7000 BCE evidence from around Palermo suggests that humans were already inhabiting the island of Sicily. Then there is a gap in the record, and the next evidence comes from between 2000 and 1100 BCE when archeologists believe that three major groups of people were living on the island from various areas of the Mediterranean. The Sicani (who inhabited the West) were believed to be the first, and they probably came from the Iberian Peninsula. The other two groups were the Sicels (who settled in the East) and the Elymians (who also settled in the West and displaced the Sicani to the center). Around 1000 BCE, Phoenician merchants started to land on the coast of the island, primarily in the West. In 814 BCE it is believed that the Phoenicians also founded a colony in Carthage (in present day Tunisia) whose residents also started settling in western Sicily.

Archeologists believe that the Greeks arrived in Sicily in the middle of the 8th century BCE, which marks the start of the island's entrance into the historical age. Since the Greek landscape was not particularly hospitable to agriculture, the Greeks were a people constantly on the hunt for more fertile land. It was this indomitable spirit of adventure that first led them to Sicily which appeared to be a rich place of opportunity; in fact, the sense of possibility Sicily offered to the Greeks in the classical period has led it to be called "the America of antiquity" by many scholars.[1] Sicily, which was called Trinacria by the Greeks (meaning three pointed island), was familiar enough to the new settlers for them to adapt easily to life there. At the same time, it was verdant enough to provide the sustainable life that many had been lacking back in their homeland.

The unusual landscape also excited the Greek imagination, to the lasting benefit of Western civilization, as their poets told stories about the treacherous spot in the Mediterranean in their myths. Homer, in fact, was referring to Sicily—specifically the straits of Messina—when he told of the double monsters Scylla and Charybdis that threatened the life of Odysseus.[2] By the time he was telling his tales, there was already a flourishing civilization in Sicily, specifically in the small Aeolian island on the northern Tyrrhenian Sea named Lipari which was one of the places that the Ithacan king visited on his epic journey.[3]

Evidence of the earliest settlements can be found on the southern coast which is a major tourist destination today as many of the ruined temples are still precariously standing.[4] Although this southern stretch of coastline boasts no natural harbors, the Greeks did not require them, because they preferred flat expanses of sand on which to beach their ships. They first were able to locate sufficiently flat beaching sites in 734 BCE in Acragas, known today as Agrigento and at Gela, in 688 BCE which was the site of one of the first American landings in Sicily during the World War II invasion.[5]

Despite this long prehistory, historians consider that the Greek period of Sicily formally began when Greek merchants established outposts for trade; the Greeks called the first colony, which

---

[1] Sammartino and Roberts, 16.

[2] The Straits of Messina are about twenty miles long and anywhere from two to twelve miles in width; the narrowest part is the famous Homeric Scylla and Charybdis.

[3] Francine Prose, *Sicilian Odyssey* (National Geographic Books, 2011), 4. {Citation}

[4] Today there are at least seven temples of the sixth and fifth centuries BCE at the site of Selinunte while Agrigento boasts nine temples. Another remarkable site is Segesta. Norwich, *Crossroads*, 5.

[5] Norwich, *Crossroads*, 4. For an account of the landing in Sicily in World War II from the perspective of a British soldier, see Ray Ward, *With the Argylls: A Soldier's Memoir* (Edinburgh, UK: Birlinn, 2014).

dates to 735 BCE, Naxos, and is located near present day Taormina on the east coast (between the northern city of Messina and the southern city of Catania). South of Catania, they soon founded Syracusae (today known as Siracusa) which between 500 BCE and 280 BCE grew to be the most powerful city in all of eastern Sicily.[6]

The Greeks were aggressive settlers who were quick to displace the indigenous inhabitants. They were not genocidal, so the displaced peoples and their cultures did survive the incursions, but the Greeks did bring much of their culture with them to Sicily. They were the ones who introduced olive and grape cultivation to the island for which the island became a valuable asset to the later Romans. Thanks to these bountiful crops, the Greeks were able to set up a dynamic, thriving community. In fact, the Greeks turned the southern coast of Sicily into one of the major centers for culture in the known world, a place where no small number of ancient poets and philosophers were able to compose their works while artists and architects flourished.[7]

In terms of military power, the only serious rivals to the Greeks was the North African city of Carthage. Carthage would make trouble for Magna Grecia, as Greek Sicily was called, and in the early 5th century, the rivalry between Carthage and Greek city states like Syracuse would spur wars inspired by competing territorial claims that often forced mass migrations of the populations.

Sicily, called Triquetra by the Romans, held a unique position in the Roman Empire, mostly due to its particular qualities at the time the Romans took control of it. On the one hand, it was geographically, ethnically and culturally diverse in and of itself, but so too was the maritime network that connected it to destinations all across the Mediterranean. This provided the Romans a rich source of relationships that they were able to put to work in their own best interest. On the other hand, as diverse and connected as it was, it was also an island and therefore was able to provide a self-contained territory that the Romans were able to administer with clearly defined borders, sparing them the trouble of having to constantly police them. Thanks to this geographical advantage, the Romans were able to effectively experiment with how to govern a colony, using Sicily as an example.[8] For the entire duration of the Roman Empire, Sicily was their central territory in the Mediterranean Sea, giving them easy access to their North African holdings. Its fertile climate also provided the Romans with abundant agricultural products, and thus became a natural center for their trading, as the Romans were able to ship valuable commodities such as grain, olive oil and wine to the Italian mainland and other Mediterranean destinations, making themselves both wealthy and indispensable.[9]

---

[6] Norwich, *Crossroads*, 4.
[7] Norwich, *Crossroads*, 4.
[8] Pfuntner, 1.
[9] Pfuntner, 2. Sicily has long been one of Italy's most important wine-producing areas, and Emperor Julius Caesar's favorite wine, Mamertino, came from the foothills of Etna. Norwich, *Crossroads*, xxvi.

The Romans turned Sicily into a vast agricultural and economic machine meant to provide grains and tax money to Rome. At the time of the conquest of Sicily, the city of Rome had a population of one million, crowded in a tiny area with relatively no agricultural activity, at most some sparse livestock. Sicily, on the contrary, had the same sized population, but they were spread out over an entire island whose fertile land could be employed to farm grain for Rome: paying taxes and farming were the main activities of the Sicilian people under the Roman Empire.[10]

Although very thorough and often insightful when it came to military and political history, most ancient Greek and Roman historians didn't dwell on administrative matters. Thus, modern knowledge of ancient administration and economy is often lacking and has to be supplemented by archaeology. Luckily in the case of Sicily, there is a very important source of information available regarding its economy and administration: Cicero's speech against the governor of Sicily, Gaius Verres (Cicero, *In Verrem*). In 70 BCE, Cicero brought a lawsuit against Verres before the Roman Senate on behalf of the Sicilian people. By adducing many testimonies and large amounts of material evidence, and by giving a detailed account of both the taxation system of the island and how Verres had abused it, Cicero finally managed to get him condemned for corruption. The fact that Verres was actually condemned by the Roman Senate shows a significant progress in the Roman rule of the island, at least when compared to the appalling conditions suffered by some under the early years of Roman rule as described in the summaries of Diodorus.

---

[10] Benjamin, chapter 3.

José Luiz Bernardes Ribeiro's picture of a bust of Cicero

    The Romans ruled (or at least claimed to rule) Sicily according to the laws of Hieron. Furthermore, different cities, according to their relationship to Rome, and especially according to whom they had sided with during the First Punic War and Second Punic War, held a different status in the eyes of Roman law and had different obligations to fulfill. Thus, some paid taxes, while others had to provide soldiers for Rome as allies. Taxes were collected according to a system of "tax farming" - in this system, the right to collect taxes from a certain area was auctioned out to private individuals by the governor (praetor) in the capital of the province. It then fell upon these private individuals and their agents to make up their loss by exacting as much tax money from the area which they had "bought" as possible. In this way, the Roman administration of the island, which was in essence little more than a stabilized military administration, received the payment upfront, and thus avoided having to maintain a bureaucracy for taxing its domains, while all the risk in the process was incurred by the tax collectors themselves. Tax farming also ensured maximum efficiency in collecting taxes, as different tax collectors could compete amongst themselves and offer higher prices in accordance to how efficiently they believed they could collect taxes and how much money they thought they could exact. The often brutal methods used by the tax collectors to exact as much money as possible from the taxpayers, exacerbated by the fact that they were acting as private individuals rather than state agents, led to widespread resentment among the populace, both in Sicily and in the rest of the Roman dominions. This bad name can even be seen in the references to tax collectors in the New Testament.

This system, implemented in Sicily, was especially important in the earliest years of Rome's rule in the Mediterranean. It served to secure a steady revenue for what, at the time, was an Italic confederacy more than an empire. But eventually, as Roman dominion spread to the rest of the Mediterranean, Sicily lost importance, especially after the conquest of Egypt in 30 BCE. After Octavian defeated Marc Antony and Cleopatra, the last Greek pharaoh of Egypt, in a civil war, he presided over the transition from the Roman Republic to the Roman Empire. In this context, Sicily would remain a peaceful, if somewhat forgotten, region of the Roman Empire for the next several centuries.

An ancient statue of Augustus

Changing Hands

Roman power in Sicily was consolidated after the Second Punic War, and Sicily remained under Rome's thumb for the entire imperial period, roughly until the Vandals started making incursions from Africa in the mid-5th century CE and damaged the island's political and economic ties to Rome. The Romans would still hold on to Sicily for a little while longer, particularly because of land ties between the island and the Church, but Roman control was no longer unequivocal.

Naturally, the fall of the Roman Empire marked a period of great change for the Sicilians, as it did for all the groups who had been part of the empire. As a result, they were subjugated by a number of foreign rulers, including Germanic groups and Ostrogoths, until the Byzantines under Justinian the Great sought to reunify the lost Roman Empire.

A contemporary mosaic depicting Justinian I

According to Procopius, the task to take back Italy from the Ostrogoths was given to General Belisarius. A rather convenient excuse for the realization of such intentions was provided by the death of the pro-Byzantine Ostrogoth queen Amalasuntha by the hands of her cousin and co-ruler Theodahad. The first attack on Theodahad and Italy was made in 535, when the armies lead by the Master of Soldiers Belisarius invaded Italy and made their way to modern-day Palermo. Theodahad was killed by his own people because of this military failure and the Ostrogoth Witigis was instituted as the new Ostrogoth king in 536. The short reign of Witigis marked the last attempt of the Ostrogoths to preserve the integrity of their Italian kingdom.

Witigis left for Ravenna after leaving a small force to guard Rome. While in Ravenna, he married Theodoric's granddaughter, Matasuntha, against her will, in order to reinforce his claims to the throne via marriage to a princess of the older dynasty. While Witigis was concentrating his forces in Ravenna, the Pope Silverius surrendered Rome to General Belisarius. Witigis retaliated in 537 with a siege on Rome and tried to cut the water supply to Belisarius' armies. Damaging the Roman aqueducts proved to be a bad move, as the water flooded Witigis' camp and turned it into a malaria infested swamp.

A contemporary mosaic believed to depict Belisarius

This military failure was followed by a three-month truce, but the Byzantine general broke the treaty by attacking Picenum. A year later, in the spring of 538, the Goths gave up on the siege of Rome. Their power was still felt in Northern Italy for two more years, despite the fact that the only haven they had was Ravenna. Ultimately, Witigis saw the solution to this military conundrum in his own abdication, after which his noblemen offered his throne to Belisarius. While giving the false illusion that he was accepting the throne as a ruler of the Ostrogoths, Belisarius entered Ravenna, after which he took Witigis and his unwilling wife Matasuntha, many on their noble retinue and what has left of Theodoric's treasure to Constantinople.[11]

The brilliant Master of Soldiers Belisarius finally got a worthy opponent in the newly appointed Ostrogoth King Totila, who ruled in the Kingdom of Italy from his ascension in the autumn of 541 until his death in 552. Totila was chosen to rule after Witigis and his retinue were taken as captives in Constantinople, but Totila proved to be quite the obstacle to Justinian's plans for uniting the old empires. By 543, through fighting on sea and land, Totila and his armies had reconquered much of Italy, but the Eternal City was holding its own and refused to surrender, despite Totila's address to the Senate demanding obedience in the name of Theodoric, to whom Rome owed alliance.

Justinian retaliated by sending Belisarius on yet another military campaign against the Goths, but in 545, Totila began a massive siege of Rome, enabled by the enlargement of his ranks with escaped Roman slaves and captives of the previous battles. Belisarius decided to try to feed the besieged city in secret instead of engaging in open battle, where he would have been outnumbered and out-resourced.[12] Nonetheless, by 546, the starved Eternal City surrendered to the hands of the Ostrogoth king. Totila showed mercy to them by not letting his soldiers violate the female population and by sending more and more food every day.

After seizing the city, Totila sent ambassadors to Justinian saying that he wished to discontinue the war and wanted to make the same arrangement with them that Theodoric had with the older Byzantine Emperors: to rule in Italy with Justinian as his overlord and to owe his alliance, armies, and taxes to Byzantium. Yet, he said that if refused, he would tear the walls of Rome to the ground and start launching raids on Illyricum.[13]

The battles between Constantinople and Totila continued off and on until the end of 550, but in 551, another of Justinian's generals, the eunuch named Narses, dealt the final blow to Totila's resistance. Narses was well respected by Justinian for his military successes, but not by his successor, Justin II, who stripped Narses of all his military honors and exiled him to Naples. As for the Ostrogoths, one of their generals named Teia was elected king after the devastating battle of Tiginae, but he did not live long enough to rule. Narses' armies killed him in the battle near

---

[11] http://www.britannica.com/EBchecked/topic/646154/Witigis.
[12] http://www.britannica.com/EBchecked/topic/600536/Totila.
[13] Bury, 1923: 244-245.

Mons Lactarius at the end of 552 or beginning of 553,[14] marking the end of the Ostrogoth resistance in Italy before it reverted completely to Byzantine control.

As for Justinian's great schemes for uniting both halves of the once great Roman Empire, things did not turn out as planned. Though he had conquered Italy, Northern Africa, and the greater portion of Gaul with the help of Belisarius and Narses, he decimated both his royal coffers and his armies in doing so. His constant war against the nations he perceived as obstacles for his plans demanded a constant influx of soldiers, and he had supplemented his ranks by retrieving troops from the Danube *limitanei* stations and leaving the northern frontier vulnerable to attacks by the Avars and Slavs. The increased taxes he imposed on the local population, who retaliated by fleeing and joining the barbarian troops instead of cultivating the land, made things even worse.

In the end, the attempt to reunite the empires was probably a futile task if only because the religious and cultural divisions that had come into existence long before were too great to be filled with an administrative merger. However, during this time, Sicily was a crossroads whose shores welcomed a variety of figures, from pilgrims, warriors, and saints to messengers and administrators, as well as immigrants looking to settle.[15] The Byzantines made eastern Siracusa the regional capital and deported many of its native inhabitants to Naples. Emperor Justinian also changed life in Sicily by devising a legal code which he imposed on the entire island, with the goal of making each of the provinces able to practice self-government. The Byzantines imported administrators, soldiers, and monks to help consolidate their power. The monks brought a formal curriculum to the island, teaching the Sicilian youth about Greek philosophy, rhetoric and music. The Byzantines also began changing the architecture of the houses of worship on the island, bringing their signature brightly colored mosaics to adorn the newly built churches.[16]

Although the Byzantines were initially more appreciated by the Sicilians than the Romans had been, inevitably this relationship soon began to sour. The Byzantine customs (such as an insistence on covering the entire body, even in extreme heat) were incompatible with the Sicilian way of life. They instituted repressive policies against women, and their pedagogical techniques were focused on rote memorization rather than open questioning. Perhaps most emblematic of all, their beloved Greek god, Dionysus, the patron saint of theater and fun, was transformed by the Byzantines into a hellish creature, and the Byzantines tried to repress any associated festivities that were important to Sicilian culture, even going so far as to refuse to baptize actors.[17]

As Byzantine power in the region faltered, Sicily became susceptible to Arab invasions, which started with random acts of piracy.[18] In 652, a small force of Muslims began to make incursions

---

[14] *Ibidem,* 250.
[15] Davis-Secord, chapter 1.
[16] Benjamin, chapter 3. On the mosaics, see Adele Cilento, *Byzantine Mosaics in Norman Sicily* (Reggio Emilia, IT: Magnus Edizioni SpA, 2019).
[17] Benjamin, chapter 3.

in Sicily, but while they were fierce and determined, they still lacked the formal organization to actually take any cities or do real damage.[19] However, by 827, the expansionist Muslims were capable of a full-blown military operation, and it would only take three years for the Arabs to take the island, with Palermo falling in 830. What they found when they took over was a culture in a profoundly decaying state.[20] The east coast city of Syracuse, which was the last main Christian outpost on the island of Sicily, held out for a longer period of time, lasting until 878 before falling to the Arab invaders.

These initial years of Muslim rule marked a turbulent period for the inhabitants of Sicily, both because of the struggles faced by the Muslim world at this time and because of their own internal conflicts.[21] After these conflicts started to die down, however, Muslim Sicily entered into a period of peace and prosperity, considered by some historians to be a cultural "golden age" for the island.[22]

Then, just as abruptly as it had started, the Arab rule of Sicily ended. The first Norman invaders arrived in Sicily in 1038, after the Arab population had already ruled the island for about 200 years.[23] The Normans originally came to Italy and Sicily in the 11th century looking for adventures and economic opportunity, but once they arrived, they found the chance for fame and fortune. Although the first Norman effort to conquer Sicily was not successful, the Norman knights quickly earned a reputation for being daring, ambitious, and resilient, bringing with them an energy that would be put to good use when they took over from the Muslims.

As the Normans gained small, informal footholds in Sicily, they likely had no idea that they were actually gathering up power for a much greater accomplishment. In 1046, the great ruler Robert Guiscard led his forces against the Muslims, and a contemporary writer provided a vivid depiction of the Norman conqueror: "This Robert was Norman by birth, of obscure origins, with an overbearing character and a thoroughly villainous mind; he was a brave fighter, very cunning in his assaults on the wealth and power of great men; in achieving his aims absolutely inexorable, diverting criticism by incontrovertible argument. He was a man of immense stature, surpassing even the biggest men; he had a ruddy complexion, fair hair, broad shoulders, eyes that all but shot out sparks of fire. In a well-built man one looks for breadth here and slimness there; in him all was admirably well-proportioned and elegant... Homer remarked of Achilles that when he shouted his hearers had the impression of a multitude in uproar, but Robert's bellow, so they say, put tens of thousands to flight."

---

[18] Karla Mallette, *The Kingdom of Sicily, 1100-1250: A Literary History* (Philadelphia, PA: University of Pennsylvania Press, 2011), 5.

[19] Benjamin, chapter 3.

[20] Karla Mallette, *The Kingdom of Sicily, 1100-1250: A Literary History* (Philadelphia, PA: University of Pennsylvania Press, 2011), 5.

[21] Mallette, 4.

[22] Mallette, 5.

[23] Mallette, 4. On the Normans, see also Mariano Marrone, *Il regno di Sicilia: dai Normanni agli Aragonesi* (Chieti, IT: Solfanelli Editore, 2014).

Merry-Joseph Blondel's painting depicting Robert Guiscard

A 14th century depiction of Robert Guiscard

In 1060, he was joined by his brother Roger, and together, the two were able to take Palermo. As a reward for his valor, Roger was made the Count of Sicily, and he took advantage of the considerable wealth there by working with the indigenous people rather than obliterating their culture.[24] This, of course, was in his best interest, insofar as he needed to consolidate his power. Since he had only a few hundred knights under his command, support from the Muslims was crucial, and he chose to treat them with respect, keeping open their mosques and naming Arabic an official language on the same footing as Latin, Greek, Norman, and French.[25] Roger Guiscard started a trend of cultural hybridism that would characterize Sicily's early development and leave an indelible mark on society.

---

[24] Mallette, 5.
[25] Norwich, Crossroads, 67.

A medieval depiction of Roger I of Sicily

A coin minted during Roger's reign that depicted him on horse

Roger ruled Sicily until his death in 1101, and his son Roger II assumed the title in 1105 when he was only nine years old. When Roger II was crowned king on Christmas Day in 1130, the "Regno" ("kingdom") of Sicily was born.[26]

---

[26] Jean Dunbabin, *The French in the Kingdom of Sicily, 1266–1305* (Cambridge, UK: Cambridge University Press,

Roger II's son, William I (r. 1154-1166), posthumously earned the title "William the Bad."[27] William II had an altogether different personality from his own father. He ruled the island from 1166-1189 and earned the title "William the Good."[28]

The Normans conquered Sicily around the same time that Christians were first seizing Muslim-occupied lands in Spain and Portugal on the Iberian Peninsula. In 1070, Palermo was conquered by the Normans, and in 1072, the Christians captured Toledo. This was a major blow to the Muslims, who struggled to survive both economically and culturally under Norman rule.[29] In fact, when the Normans conquered Sicily, they not only took possession of the abundant natural resources of the island, but they also came to control its vast cultural production and its advanced bureaucratic and cultural institutions.[30] As a result, the Normans inadvertently ended up merging Islamic art, literature and architecture in the service of a Christian king.[31] They also brought together Arabic, Greek and Latin, to develop a language of bureaucracy and of culture.[32] During the Norman rule, court poets in Sicily actually composed their poetic verses in Arabic.

12th century Sicily was a time of intense cultural exchange. The island was now inhabited by Normans, Byzantine Greeks, Arabs, Germans, and Jews, making it a paragon of cultural diversity. At the intersection of Europe, Africa, and Asia, this culture flourished and proved to be greater than the sum of its parts. In addition to the commonplace occurrence of bilingualism, it was a time when the rights of women were honored, and there were signs of respect for the environment that predated contemporary environmentalist movements by nearly 1,000 years. Sicilians during this time were uncommonly literate, so much so that 700 years later, the island's literacy rates would be markedly lower than they were during this remarkable golden age.[33]

Unfortunately, this period was relatively short lived. When William II "The Good" died in 1189, he became "William the Lamented."[34] His death caused Sicily to fall into a period of confusion and discord that ultimately brought the Norman-Sicilian experimentation to an abrupt end.[35] This was due to the rise of Frederick II, who, despite being a great ruler and considered no less tolerant than his father, was much more interested in establishing strong ties between Sicily and Europe rather than the Muslim world, particularly in terms of cultural production.[36] As a

---

2011), 19.

[27] According to Norwich, he was given this nickname two hundred years after his death, somewhat undeservedly: first, because he never managed to live up to his beloved father and second, the principle historian of his reign, Falcandus, passionately hated him. Furthermore, Norwich claims that he was apparently quite ugly, large and with a savage looking beard although no portraits of him survive. Norwich, *Crossroads*, 80.

[28] Mallette, 5.

[29] Mallette, 3.

[30] Mallette, 3-4.

[31] Mallette, 4.

[32] Mallette, 5.

[33] Louis Mendola and Jacqueline Alio, *The Peoples of Sicily: A Multicultural Legacy* (Palermo, It: Trinacria Editions, 2014).

[34] Mallette, 47.

[35] Mallette, 5.

result, in the late 12th century, the poets of Sicily began to write in a vernacular that was much closer to that which was being used in the Italian mainland. This ultimately produced the dialect that would come to be known as Sicilian.[37]

A contemporary bust of Frederick II

It is safe to say that Frederick II was responsible for another apex in the history of Sicily. Generally recognized as the finest monarch of the Middle Ages, Frederick was responsible for founding the universities of Naples and Padua, and he developed Sicilian forms of governance.[38] He technically ascended to the throne at the age of three, and he began to directly govern at the age of 14 in 1208. At 26, he became Holy Roman Emperor in 1220 following a coronation at St. Peter's in Rome.[39] Truly cosmopolitan, he was fluent in five languages[40] and had Norman, German, and Sicilian lineage. He had a diverse court of people surrounding him, including

[36] Mallette, 6.
[37] Mallette, 4.
[38] Monroe, 79-80.
[39] Jeremy Dummett, *Palermo, City of Kings: The Heart of Sicily* (London ; New York: I.B.Tauris, 2015), 63.
[40] Matthews, 113-114.

Saracen bodyguards and Jewish advisers. He also was born into a highly unstable, turbulent climate, and learned at an early age not to trust the people around him.[41] Historian Donald Detwiler wrote of him, "A man of extraordinary culture, energy, and ability – called by a contemporary chronicler stupor mundi (the wonder of the world), by Nietzsche the first European, and by many historians the first modern ruler – Frederick established in Sicily and southern Italy something very much like a modern, centrally governed kingdom with an efficient bureaucracy."

One of the most remarkable aspects of Frederick II's reign was his court, the place where poets invented the sonnet and developed the Italian vernacular known as the "Sicilian form."[42] In the early 1230s, a group of courtiers experimented with poems on the themes of love, and this came to be known as the Sicilian school. Their poetry was a great source of inspiration for medieval Italian poets such as Dante and Petrarch, but their influence also spread across Europe and even inspired Shakespeare and Milton.[43] Frederick II's devotion to culture was in keeping with his intellectual upbringing. In fact, he himself was an accomplished author, writing a treatise on falcons that gets referenced by falconers to this day.

During this new golden age of Sicily, Palermo was the capital of Frederick's reign, but he tried to extend his reach beyond to Italy, France, Germany, and even the Holy Land, where his attempts at diplomacy (rather than military aggression) angered Pope Innocent IV and led to his excommunication.[44]

---

[41] Dummett, 63.

[42] Matthew, 113.

[43] Dummett, 66. Although Dante obviously admired Frederick II and his court, he placed him in hell in his epic poem, *The Divine Comedy,* because of his tumultuous relationship with the pope that resulted in his ex-communication.

[44] Farrell, *Sicily: A Cultural History*.

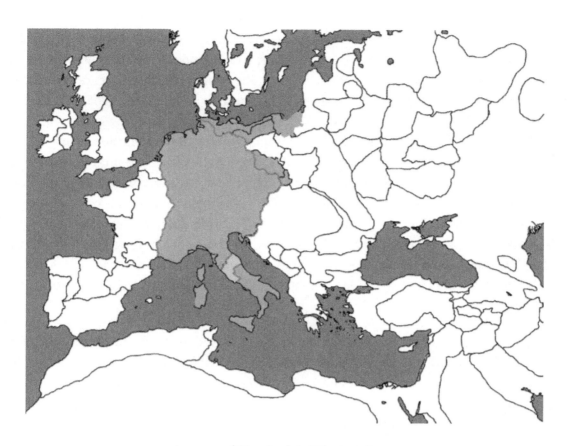

A map of Frederick II's territory

A medieval depiction of Frederick II's excommunication

For all the celebration of Frederick II's enlightened attitude, he was not entirely egalitarian when it came to ethnic persecution. He relocated the Muslim population to Puglia when they revolted against him, a sign that his powers were on the wane.[45] Furthermore, despite the prolific cultural mixing that occurred during his reign, there was a clear hierarchy. The Greeks, for example, lived fairly peaceably in the kingdom and were accepted insofar as they were Christians, yet they were clearly second-class citizens compared to the Latins. Some historians even go so far as to say that there was no official interest in inspiring the mixing of cultures, and that it was more a result of happenstance that proved to be a transitory phenomenon.[46] In fact, by the time of Frederick II's death in 1250, Latin culture was the dominant force in the Kingdom of Sicily, the number of Arabic-speaking inhabitants had sharply declined, and the Greeks had dwindled in number and in prosperity.[47] The only exception to this homogenization was the population of Jews, which remained robust. They worked as scholars and translators, acting as a bridge between the Arabic-speaking inhabitants and the Latin population. They also cultivated silk and indigo.[48]

Even as the Kingdom of Sicily started homogenizing its identity, it continued to look abroad for trading and political relations. Located practically in the center of the Mediterranean Sea, it was an important port of call for traders, and its fertile climate meant that it had much in the way of desirable exports, including grains, vegetables, olive oil, raw cotton, and silk. They traded with North Africa as well as the cities of Italy.[49]

The Early Modern Period and the Bourbons

Frederick II was the last ruler of a fully autonomous Sicily, and his son, Manfred (r. 1254-1258), was the final Norman ruler in Sicily. Manfred met his death heroically on the battlefield, fighting the army of Charles of Anjou after Charles was made King of Rome by the pope in 1266.[50] Charles chose Naples as the capital of his lands, and this created tensions between his people and the Sicilians, culminating with a rebellion known as the Sicilian Vespers of 1282. According to legend, the rebellion started after a French soldier harrassed a Sicilian woman on Easter Sunday outside the Church of Santo Spirito.

However it came about, the rebellion inaugurated a period of anarchy in Sicily, and for a time was unclear who would take the crown. Two warring factions, the Aragonese and the Angevins, competed for the crown for 90 years, to the detriment of all involved. At one point, there were two different kings of Sicily, one from each side, and it was not until 1372 that peace was finally reached and the Aragonese were awarded rule of Sicily. As a result of all this geopolitical

---

[45] Mallette, 56.
[46] Matthew, 112.
[47] Dunbabin, 20.
[48] Dunbabin, 21.
[49] Dunbabin, 21.
[50] Monroe, 80-81.

turmoil, Sicily's status in the world was greatly diminished. Spain was on the rise, and even if Palermo received certain bureaucratic dispensations, nothing would shift the center of power back into Sicily's orbit. [51]

In the wake of the infighting, Sicily was affected by other major geopolitical events elsewhere. When Constantinople fell in 1453, the ascent of the Ottoman Turks meant that Sicily was constantly being threatened. Pirates and corsairs from North Africa continued to besiege the coastal towns, and the island became an important staging ground for those trying to counter the Muslims.[52]

In 1469, the crowns of Aragon and Castile were coordinated with the marriage of Ferdinand and Isabella,[53] and a dark period began for the Sicilians. While much of Europe experienced a flourishing culture during the Renaissance, the 15th and 16th centuries in Sicily were completely cut off from all the cultural and technological advances, despite the fact Italy was the epicenter of everything. Moreover, thanks to Spain's Catholic zeal, Sicily faced the worst excesses of the Counter-Reformation.[54]

Ferdinand and Isabella

Though nominally in control, the Spanish Empire was more interested in the Americas, so it left Sicily to its own devices, rarely for better, and frequently for worse. By the 1700s, the island

---

[51] Farrell, *Sicily: A Cultural History*.
[52] For example, the Christian fleet departed from Messina, Sicily, in 1453, on their way to fight in the important Battle of Lepanto against the Turks.
[53] Farrell, *Sicily: A Cultural History*.
[54] Farrell, Sicily: A Cultural History.

of Sicily was nothing resembling what it once did, relegated instead to being a mere pawn in geopolitics. Nothing underscores Sicily's position more than the 1713 Treaty of Utrecht,[55] in which the Spanish offered Sicily to the Duke of Savoy only for the offer to be rejected. In 1720, the island was given to the Austrians, but when they lost the War of the Polish Succession,[56] it passed back to the Spanish. At the time, Spain was ruled by the Bourbon King Don Carlos, who had been crowned in Palermo on July3, 1735 as King Charles III.[57]

Charles III of Spain

In 1743, control of Sicily transitioned one more time when the Spanish crown passed it to the Neapolitan Bourbons, who mostly managed to stay in power until 1860, when Sicily was

---

[55] *Sicily and England. A Sketch of Events in Sicily in 1812 & 1848. Illustrated by Vouchers and State Papers* (London: James Ridgway, 1849), iii–iv.

[56] Giovanni Evangelista di Blasi e Gambacorta, *Storia civile del regno di Sicilia* (Palermo, It: Reale Stamperia, 1818).

[57] Farrell, *Sicily: A Cultural History.*

incorporated into a united Italy during the Risorgimento. What seemed like a good idea on paper proved complex, however. Naples and Sicily had similar cultural and economic characteristics, as well as kinship and matrimonial ties between their aristocratic classes. The Neapolitan elite were happy about the arrangement, as it turned Naples into the capital of an independent kingdom. In fact, the rulers intended to reform the province of Sicily during the Enlightenment, believing the island needed to have public finances, tax codes, and confused fiscal policies fixed.

Of course, the preexisting systems were in place to serve the interests of the ruling Sicilian barons.[58] While the barons lived a good life, living conditions in Sicily at this time were basically primitive, with precarious dwellings perched on unstable land, all under the unforgiving gaze of the barons and their domineering castles.[59] The Bourbons sought to undermine the power of the Sicilian barons, both politically and economically, figuring that once they were weakened, they could be replaced with a single, centralized authority stationed in Naples.[60]

Not surprisingly, the Bourbons' intentions to reform Sicily was met with serious resistance on the part of the barons, who denied that they owed any taxes to the crown.[61] The barons were deeply entrenched in their societal milieu, and they were determined not to cede any ground, a theme that would persist throughout the history of the island. It was one of Sicily's great writers, Giuseppe Tomasi di Lampedusa, in his celebrated novel *The Leopard,* who captured the essence of the era: "If we want things to stay as they are, things will have to change."[62]

Ultimately, the Bourbons did have some success in weakening the old noble class with their reforms, yet they also inadvertently worked to foment a revolutionary atmosphere that was to cost them.[63] Although Sicily was generally cut off from Europe, that did not stop the ideas and the spirit of the French Revolution from reaching Sicilian shores. In fact, when Napoleon and his army stormed Naples in 1798, the island could not keep itself immune from the tides of change. Considering all the invasions Sicily withstood throughout its long history, it is somewhat ironic that the Sicilians would not physically experience the biggest French invasion in history, even as Napoleon permanently changed the course of Italy's destiny. In fact, Sicily ended up becoming a place of refuge for the dethroned Bourbons once they were exiled from Naples.[64]

---

[58] Fentress, 15.
[59] Fentress, 17.
[60] Riall, 25.
[61] Fentress, 18.
[62] "Essay: Lampedusa's 'The Leopard,' Fifty Years on - The New York Times," accessed April 30, 2019, https://www.nytimes.com/2008/07/29/arts/29iht-booktue.1.14826755.html.Giuseppe Tomasi di Lampedusa, *The Leopard* (New York: Pantheon Books, 1960).
[63] Riall, 26.
[64] Farrell, Sicily: A Cultural History. See also Giovanni Evangelista di Blasi, *Storia del regno di Sicilia* (Palermo, It: Edizioni Dafni, 1847).

Napoleon

King Ferdinand IV of Naples was celebrated upon his arrival in Palermo in December 1798, as it appeared to be a sign of the city's prestige, but it soon became clear that he intended to use Palermo as a source of income to finance his reconquest of Naples. Eight years later, when King Ferdinand IV was forced to escape Naples and flee to Palermo once more, he found an icy welcome on the part of the Sicilian aristocracy, and this time he was only able to rule thanks to the support he received from the British government. The Sicilians' diffidence towards the Spanish rulers was quite justifiable, and the Bourbons continued to display no gratitude towards the city or the island that had hosted them during the Napoleonic Era.[65] When they were restored to power after Waterloo, they enacted reactionary policies in Sicily that fomented social unrest, and their myopic, self-centered leadership ensured that Sicily mostly missed out on the benefits of the Industrial Revolution. Thus, the quality of living remained at extremely low standards

---

[65] Fentress, 19.

during the early 19th century.

King Ferdinand IV of Naples

Italian Unification

Sicily started the 19th century as a Spanish holding and ended it as a part of the Italian nation, but the fact that Sicily went through three different regimes over the course of the 19th century has risked obscuring a fundamental source of continuity throughout. In fact, historians tend to forget that the Bourbon monarchy, the dictatorship of Giuseppe Garibaldi, and the unified Italian government all displayed similar attitudes towards Sicily, adopted similar policies towards the island, and enacted them poorly. They all attempted to try to control the island not by making a formalized, centralized apparatus, but by making informal bargains with the local aristocratic class. The fact that three different kinds of rulers all tried and failed to govern Sicily suggests there was something wrong with the governing strategies, not the Sicilians themselves, but nonetheless, the island earned itself the unfair reputation of being veritably ungovernable. Amongst the Italian liberal government, it was considered a place where ambition went to die, and where all efforts of reform were due to failure because of the violent, impenetrable nature of the society. Neither bureaucrats nor soldiers could bring Sicily into the fold.[66] Northerners

---

[66] Riall, 1.

blamed these failures on the nature of the Sicilian people themselves; as organized crime began to flourish, they thought that the newly formed shadow state was a vestige of its medieval past that had yet to die. However, the northerners themselves were in large part to blame, for they lacked an understanding of the people they were seeking to incorporate, and they were also attempting to incorporate the Sicilians as subordinates.

In the years before unification, Sicilian society was in constant turmoil. In 1812, nervous nobles decided to draw up a constitution which declared Sicily an independent state to be ruled by its own monarch.[67] They even created a parliamentary system with representation for the different regions as well as the church. However, they proved ineffectual at governing, and in 1816, the kingdoms of Naples and of Sicily were officially merged to form the Kingdom of the Two Sicilies, governed by none other than the despised King Ferdinand IV of Naples.

Initially, this appeared to be a satisfactory compromise because the Sicilians expected to maintain their autonomy regardless, but instead, the situation brought about major revolts in 1820 and in 1830, after which Ferdinand II ascended to the throne.

---

[67] Gregory, *Sicily. Sicily and England. A Sketch of Events in Sicily in 1812 & 1848. Illustrated by Vouchers and State Papers.*

Ferdinand II of the Two Sicilies

Then, in 1837, further riots ignited on the island.[68] Although they were called the cholera riots, the cause was not just the spread of the deadly disease but also about Italian independence and unification, alongside the festering problem of slow economic growth. The revolts brought together Sicilians of all classes, and though they did not succeed, it foreshadowed the bigger changes that were to come in the next decade.[69]

In 1848, the island attempted to declare its independence, coming during a year that marked widespread revolt and revolution throughout the entire European continent. In this, Palermo was at the forefront as students at the university began rioting, and the whole island was quickly caught up in the spirit of protest. The successful uprising of 1848 then served to ignite in the hearts of Sicilians the desire for unification that would come in just twelve short years.[70]

When Giuseppe Garibaldi landed in Marsala, Sicily in 1860 with his 1,000 volunteers (known as Redshirts), he declared an end to Bourbon rule and declared that Sicily would be a part of the new Italian nation under his rule.[71] Palermo formally became an Italian city on June 7, 1860, and the withdrawal of the Bourbon forces from the harbor constituted one of the greatest military achievements of the century, astonishing the rest of Europe.[72] Just four months later, Garibaldi went from his conquest of Palermo to the whole of Southern Italy, after which he began preparing to take Rome from the pope and make it the capital of a united Italian nation.

---

[68] Samuel Kline Cohn, *Epidemics: Hate and Compassion from the Plague of Athens to AIDS* (Oxford, UK: Oxford University Press, 2018), 182. The epidemic is also recounted in an early edition of *Baedekers, Southern Italy and Sicily: With Excursions to Malta, Sardinia, Tunis, and Corfu; Handbook for Travellers* (K. Baedeker, 1908), 271.

[69] Sammartino, 104.

[70] Sammartino, 104.

[71] Denis Mack Smith, *Modern Italy: A Political History* (Ann Arbor, MI: University of Michigan Press, 1997), 23.

[72] John Dickie, *Cosa Nostra: A History of the Sicilian Mafia* (New York: St. Martin's Press, 2015), 35.

Garibaldi

In many ways, it is fair to argue that the seeds of Italian unification (known in Italy as the *Risorgimento* or "resurgence") were planted in Sicily, yet its role as a point of origin did nothing to make the process of unification any smoother for the fiercely independent island.[73] Mainland Italians, particularly from the north, did not know what to make of their new countrymen. They discovered in Sicily a land with low standards of living dependent on an agricultural economy. That was certainly true, but Sicily's new rulers also were blinded by stereotypes and prejudices.[74] Prime Minister Camillo Benso Cavour even told Parliament that he believed Sicilians spoke Arabic.[75]

---

[73] Riall, 1. On Sicily in the Risorgimento, see also Rosario Romeo, *Il Risorgimento in Sicilia* (Rome: Laterza Editore, 1973).

[74] On the various myths and stereotypes about Sicily, see Giuseppe Giarrizzo, *Mezzogiorno senza meridionalismo: la Sicilia, lo sviluppo, il potere* (Venice: Marsilio Editore, 1992).

[75] Caroline Moorehead, *Human Cargo: A Journey Among Refugees* (New York: Henry Holt and Company, 2007), 76.

This kind of ignorant attitude on the part of the ruling class was sometimes openly hostile and sometimes veiled with romantic attachment, but through it all, it was to characterize the entire process of incorporation of Sicily into the Italian state and would directly contribute to the rise of the Sicilian Mafia.[76] Many Sicilians resented the interventions of northerners, who were said to have brought to the island just two things: taxation and mandatory military service. Following unification, emigration rates skyrocketed in Sicily as many Sicilians sought to flee poverty and conscription. The question of taxation was particularly vexing, insofar as the people tended to believe that the fact that they had overthrown the Bourbons through a patriotic rebellion should have somehow exempted them from paying taxes.[77]

Another unanticipated problem was caused by the change in the economic system that occurred when the Bourbon government was dismantled. The Bourbons had actually favored the poor in their economic policies, for instance by depressing the cost of bread via a prohibition on exporting grain. As a result, when a free market was created after 1861, agricultural prices naturally rose. This was considered economic progress as Sicily was inducted into a free trade market rather than depending on a paternalistic system; but the dramatic change in policy affected the poorest members of society in a devastating fashion, which served to create widespread resentment towards the newly formed Italian state.[78]

By 1866, the Italian government was facing another revolt in Palermo, one eerily resembling the rebellion that had defeated the Bourbons. Revolutionary gangs descended upon the city, using the surrounding hills as their camps. Public fear was at a high, as rumors of cannibalism and blood drinking (albeit uncorroborated) flew through the city. The Italian government responded by imposing martial law, but it took an entire decade before Sicily managed to incorporate itself functionally into the Italian state. Finally, in 1876, its politicians were able to enter into a new coalition government in Rome.[79]

As bad as things were during the second half of the 19th century, new visitors to the city, including some of the members of the Italian army, could not help but be amazed by its splendors.[80] Although most foreign destinations become reflections of the visitors' own image, Sicily is a place that most acutely excites the fears and strengthens the preconceived beliefs of its visitors. In the 18th century, aristocrats made Sicily a stop on their grand tour, flocking to Mount Etna and sites of ancient Greek and Roman ruins such as Taormina, Syracuse, and Agrigento. Others, who were more erudite, actually used their trips to Sicily to pursue an interest in natural science and take advantage of the prehistoric caves, advancing their understanding of geology. Some were able to study the unparalleled volcanic evidence provided by Etna and by Stromboli.[81]

---

[76] Gino Bedani and B. A. Haddock, *The Politics of Italian National Identity: A Multidisciplinary Perspective* (Cardiff, UK: University of Wales Press, 2000), 93.
[77] Dickie, 36.
[78] Mack Smith, 35.
[79] Dickie, 37.
[80] Dickie, 37.

Some of the most famous visitors to Sicily were writers who were inspired by their travels to Sicily and wrote unforgettable descriptions of the island. In addition to Goethe, some writers inspired by Sicily include Henry Swinburne, Edward Lear, Alexandre Dumas, Guy de Maupassant,[82] D.H. Lawrence[83] and E.M. Forster.[84] These modern writers were attracted by the same place that inspired ancient Greek and Arab poets.[85] Winston Churchill even sought refuge in Sicily during his retirement, traveling to Siracusa to reflect on its ancient history.[86]

Visitors were understandably drawn in by the drama of Palermo's scenery, with walls that were encircled by olive and lemon groves and surrounded by a veritable amphitheater of hills and mountains.[87] As foreigners got to know the city, they were only more enthralled. Northern European visitors to Sicily were impressed with the delicious cuisine, and Goethe noted, "The vegetables are delicious, especially the lettuce, which is very tender and tastes like milk… The oil and the wine are also good, but would be even better if prepared with greater care. The fish – excellent and of a most delicate flavor. We have always had good beef, too, though most people here do not recommend it."[88] People were thrilled by the island's climate, with its seemingly unending summers and temperate evenings that the locals spent taking carriage rides along the harbor. They appreciated the myriad houses of worship and diversity of monuments left behind by the countless invaders, including Greek temples, Roman villas, Arab mosques and gardens, Norman cathedrals, Renaissance palaces, and baroque churches. The list of attractions was (and still is) almost countless.[89]

However, as is so often the case with Sicily, it was a place of dramatic contrasts, including beauty and devastation. While the coastal cities like Palermo, as well as eastern Catania and Siracusa, Southern Agrigento and Western Trapani, were sources of delight, the inland area was devastatingly barren. In 1943, when the Allies prepared to invade Sicily and wrest control of it from the Axis, a pamphlet warned soldiers not be taken in by Sicily's outward appearance of beauty, and to be mindful of the fact that the interior of the island was still completely underdeveloped.[90]

---

[81] Leighton, 1.

[82] Guy de Maupassant's travelogue from his trip to Sicily in 1885 has been translated from French into English, and provides a compelling account of what he described as a "strange and divine museum of architecture," Guy de Maupassant, *Sicily* (New York: Italica Press, 2007).

[83] Carmine Rapisarda, *British and American Writers in Sicily* (Raleigh, NC: Lulu.com, 2012), 1. On D.H. Lawrence's travels to Sicily, see Carmine Rapisarda, *David Herbert Lawrence and Sicily* (Raleigh, NC: Lulu.com, 2012).

[84] For an account of an unknown English woman traveling in Sicily, see Helen Lowe, *Unprotected Females in Sicily, Calabria, and on the Top of Mount Aetna* (London: Routledge, Warnes and Routledge, 1859).

[85] Joseph Farrell, *Sicily: A Cultural History* (Northampton, MA: Interlink Publishing Group, Incorporated, 2013).

[86] Edward Chaney, *The Evolution of the Grand Tour: Anglo-Italian Cultural Relations since the Renaissance* (London: Routledge, 2014).

[87] Dickie, 37.

[88] Goethe, *Italian Journey, 1786-1788*, 247.

[89] Dickie, 37.

[90] *Soldier's Guide to Sicily* (Printing and Stationery Services, M.E.F., 1943).

A picture of Allied troops unloading supplies during the invasion of Sicily

The Allied operations on Sicily would bring about Mussolini's downfall, his imprisonment, and subsequent dramatic rescue by the scar-faced Otto Skorzeny, removing significant portions of Italy from the fascist camp, but it all came at a heavy cost. On paper, Sicily's garrison appeared as a formidable obstacle to the Allies' plans, but in actuality, most of the resistance came from the small number of German troops on the island. The vast numbers of Italian soldiers accomplished little other than to flee or surrender en masse, but even this delayed the Allied forces long enough for Hitler to greatly reinforce the Wehrmacht in Italy. In the memorable words of a war correspondent, the campaign resembled "a thirty-eight day race with the Italians in the lead."

In fact, the lackluster Allied showing on Sicily and the escape of most of the island's garrison encouraged Hitler to alter his plans and defend Italy vigorously. With its rugged mountain ridges, deep valleys, and numerous rivers, Italy contained tens of thousands of natural defensive positions. The Wehrmacht exploited these to the full during the ensuing campaign, bogging down the Allied armies in an endless series of costly, time-consuming engagements. Even the rank and file German soldiers showed a clear awareness of the Italy's strategic significance, as one anecdote related by historian Max Hastings makes clear: "'The Tommies will have to chew their way through us inch by inch,' a German paratrooper wrote in an unfinished letter found on his corpse at Salerno, 'and we will surely make hard chewing for them.'"

The Sicilian Mafia

Over the course of the 19th century, the people of Sicily found themselves at the center of a struggle for freedom, one that ended up being long and often very bloody.[91] It was during these crucial years of struggle that the Sicilian mafia, *La cosa nostra* ("Our thing"), started to take shape.[92] The original word "mafia" was a part of Palermitan slang, and although the origins of the word are not completely certain, some linguistic historians believe it originally meant "flashy."[93] One historian of the mafia, Salvatore Lupo, helpfully suggests that it was used in its earliest iterations to vaguely refer to a "pathological relationship among politics, society and criminality."[94]

In response to the rise of the mafia, the Italian state propagated a doctrine of Sicilian backwardness,[95] which they used to introduce martial law and suspend civil liberties, under the pretext that they were not "ready" for the freedoms enjoyed by other Italian regions.[96] Northerners and foreigners mistakenly (and snobbishly) believed that the mafia was just a relic of the primitive, peasant culture that had dominated the island for centuries, and that it was destined to die out once the island had been properly absorbed into the dominant, mainland culture. Others hypothesized that the corruption in Sicilian culture was just a holdover from the Bourbon government and would soon be extinguished once a formal transition was completed.[97]

Of course, they proved to be dead wrong.[98] The Sicilian mafia was not a criminal underworld or a form of political rebellion, but more of a kingdom within a kingdom. In other words, according to historians of the mafia, it was a network of hidden power, an alternative hierarchy that sometimes worked in concert with and sometimes superseded official forms of law and order.[99]

What gets forgotten in all the flashy Hollywood portrayals of dapper, violent men with greasy hair is that the first area in which the mafia developed its methods was in the citrus fruit industry. Sworn testimony from a respected surgeon, a man named Gaspare Galati, provides the details of how the mafia developed its techniques through the blossoming citrus industry. A prized Sicilian

---

[91] James Fentress, *Rebels and Mafiosi: Death in a Sicilian Landscape* (Ithaca, NY: Cornell University Press, 2018), 5. To give some context to the unique nature of Sicily's criminality during the early nineteenth century, brigandage was a problem throughout mainland Italy; however, after 1865, it had more or less been brought under control – except on the island. Riall, 4.

[92] Dickie, 38.

[93] Fentress, 6.

[94] Salvatore Lupo, *History of the Mafia* (New York: Columbia University Press, 2011), 31.

[95] On the history of "backwardness" as a paradigm for northern rule of Sicily, see Riall, esp. introduction.

[96] Fentress, 7.

[97] Riall, 2.

[98] Lupo, *History of the Mafia*.

[99] Fentress, 7.

export since the late 1700s when the British Royal Navy began to buy them as a cure for scurvy, by 1834 Sicily was exporting 400,000 cases of lemons to New York. That number grew to 750,000 by 1850 and to 2.5 million cases by the mid-1880s. This made Sicilian lemon groves the most profitable agricultural land in Europe.

The lemon groves, however, required a large initial investment to get the trees planted and eight years before they were able to bear fruit. They are also vulnerable trees at constant risk of vandalism. As such, the high profit margins and high levels of risk ensured the industry was a perfect setting for the protection rackets that made the Cosa Nostra famous. Another important factor to remember when tracing the relationship between the development of the mafia and the citrus industry is that both were predominantly a western Sicilian phenomenon, taking shape in the area surrounding Palermo, Sicily's most populous center with 200,000 inhabitants in 1861.[100]

When Dr. Galati was called upon to manage his daughters' inheritance, he began to receive threatening letters, and suspicion was cast upon the wardens he had hired to manage the lemon grove. According to police investigation, these wardens were being employed by the mafia, and they used their considerably powerful threats to try to coerce Dr. Galati into paying for their protection. Dr. Galati did go to the authorities about these threats, but they were mostly helpless, and Galati ended up fleeing to Naples to escape the threat of death.[101]

From these humble origins, the mafia grew quickly, to the extent that by 1890, the Cosa Nostra had already developed into a sophisticated criminal organization with a great deal of blood on its hands. In fact, its tentacles reached into the highest levels of politics and beyond the borders of Sicily and Italy, traveling across the Atlantic to the United States.[102] Today, their power has been dwarfed by the Neapolitan mafia, La Camorra, yet the Cosa Nostra has continued to wreak havoc in Sicily. In 1992 they were responsible for one of the most high-profile assassinations in Italy since the fall of fascism. Members detonated a bomb with 400 kilograms of explosives that targeted Judge Giovanni Falcone, who had been responsible for mafia convictions.[103]

Ironically, the murderous actions of a small segment of society have caused the Sicilian people in general to be perceived as "Mafiosi,"[104] even though the vast majority of them have been victims rather than perpetrators.

Sicily's Legacy

Throughout these centuries of tumult and change, Sicily was fortunate to have an active literary culture, comprised of men and women who wanted to use their literary talents to call attention to

---

[100] Dickie, 39.
[101] Nigel Cawthorne, *Mafia: The History of the Mob* (Arcturus Publishing, 2012).
[102] Dickie, 15.
[103] Dickie, 14.
[104] Dickie, 16.

the dire conditions of the island. One of Italy's greatest writers was Giovanni Verga, a writer who engaged with the dynamic cultural landscape in order to forge a new, unique literary style known as *verismo* (roughly translated as realism). Inspired by the French literary movement of naturalism, *verismo* looked at modest subjects, including peasants, and tried to take an objective, even scientific narrative position. There was a social component to *verismo,* as it sought to call attention to the plight of the lower classes while at the same time exhibiting no small degree of paternalism. Verga is the most famous of the practitioners of *verismo,* but he was not alone. Another well-known writer of *verismo* was Luigi Capuana, while the most famous Sicilian woman writer in this genre is Maria Messina.[105]

Verga

While Italy has not had a large number of Nobel Prize winners in literature, Sicily boasts two, thanks to the modernist playwright Luigi Pirandello[106] and the hermetic poet Salvatore Quasimodo. [107] Two other most famous Sicilian writers, beloved throughout Italy, are Leonardo Sciascia and Andrea Camilleri, who looked unflinchingly at the most secretive aspects of Sicilian culture, including the mafia. Finally, although Sicily by and large adhered to Mussolini's regime during the fascist era, Sicily also was home to two of Italy's most prominent antifascist writers,

---

[105] Maria Messina, *Behind Closed Doors: Her Father's House and Other Stories of Sicily* (New York: The Feminist Press at CUNY, 2007).
[106] Luigi Pirandello, *Pirandello's Major Plays* (Evanston, IL: Northwestern University Press, 1991).
[107] Salvatore Quasimodo and Jack Bevan, *Complete Poems* (New York: Schocken Books, 1984).

Elio Vittorini, and Vitaliano Brancati.[108] Brancati's anti-fascist satire *Il bell'Antonio* is the most translated postwar Italian novel, having been translated into English three different times.

Brancati

Stereotypes about Sicily and Sicilians abound, but if there is one thread that runs throughout the knotty history of Sicily, it is diversity. For all the violence and turmoil that plagued the island, the countless invaders left behind a rich cultural tapestry visible in the striking artistic and architectural heritage of the island. The island has been inhabited by Phoenicians, Greeks, Vandals, Goths, Romans, Arabs, Berbers, Franks, Normans, and various Christians, Muslims and Jews. While the diversity of its inhabitants was always known, today there is the science to back it up - according to recent DNA analyses, the population of Sicily today is extremely genetically diverse.

Through all these invasions - indeed, because of them - Sicilian identity has been well defined, managing to be both diverse and also somehow rather strikingly identifiable. Sicilian cuisine, with its extremes of sweet and spicy, is one of Italy's most well defined. So too are the symbols of the island, from the little red chili peppers meant to bring good luck to the ancient Trinacria at the center of the Sicilian flag (the head of Medusa overlaying three legs conjoined at the hips and flexed in a triangle and three stalks of wheat). Unfortunately, so is the *Cosa Nostra,* an Italian export that made Italian-American immigrants hated and feared when they immigrated to the United States.[109]

It remains a puzzle how it could be that Sicily seems so diverse, so distinct from Italy, so "other," and yet also somehow becomes synonymous with the boot-shaped nation it so

---

[108] Guido Bonsaver, *Elio Vittorini: The Writer and the Written* (New York: Routledge, 2017).Vitaliano Brancati, *Antonio, the Great Lover*, trans. Vladimir Kean (D. Dobson, 1952).

[109] George De Stefano, *An Offer We Can't Refuse: The Mafia in the Mind of America* (New York: Faber & Faber/Farrar, Straus, Giroux, 2007). See also, Peter Robb, *Midnight In Sicily: On Art, Food, History, Travel and La Cosa Nostra* (New York: Farrar, Straus and Giroux, 2014).

problematically joined. Perhaps the only answer can be that Italy itself is a paradox and Sicily, thus, is Italy in miniature.

Online Resources

<u>Other books about Italian history by Charles River Editors</u>

<u>Other books about Sicily on Amazon</u>

Bibliography

Abulafia, David. *The Great Sea: A Human History of the Mediterranean*. Oxford University Press, USA, 2011.

————. *The Mediterranean in History*. London: Getty Publications, 2011.

Bedani, Gino, and B. A. Haddock. *The Politics of Italian National Identity: A Multidisciplinary Perspective*. Cardiff, UK: University of Wales Press, 2000.

Block, Richard A. *The Spell of Italy: Vacation, Magic, and the Attraction of Goethe*. Detroit, MI: Wayne State University Press, 2006.

Bonsaver, Guido. *Elio Vittorini: The Writer and the Written*. New York: Routledge, 2017.

Brancati, Vitaliano. *Antonio, the Great Lover*. Translated by Vladimir Kean. D. Dobson, 1952.

Brown, Gordon S. *The Norman Conquest of Southern Italy and Sicily*. Jefferson, NC: McFarland Publishers, 2015.

Camilleri, Andrea. *A Nest of Vipers*. Penguin, 2017.

Cawthorne, Nigel. *Mafia: The History of the Mob*. Arcturus Publishing, 2012.

Chaney, Edward. *The Evolution of the Grand Tour: Anglo-Italian Cultural Relations since the Renaissance*. London: Routledge, 2014.

Cilento, Adele. *Byzantine Mosaics in Norman Sicily*. Reggio Emilia, IT: Magnus Edizioni SpA, 2019.

Cohn, Samuel Kline. *Epidemics: Hate and Compassion from the Plague of Athens to AIDS*. Oxford, UK: Oxford University Press, 2018.

Davies, Judith. *The Realism of Luigi Capuana: Theory and Practice in the Development of Late Nineteenth-Century Italian Narrative*. London: The Modern Humanities Research Association, 1979.

Davis-Secord, Sarah. *Where Three Worlds Met: Sicily in the Early Medieval Mediterranean*. Cornell, NY: Cornell University Press, 2017.

Di-Blasi, Giovanni Evangelista. *Storia del regno di Sicilia*. Palermo, It: Edizioni Dafni, 1847.

Dickie, John. *Cosa Nostra: A History of the Sicilian Mafia*. New York: St. Martin's Press, 2015.

Dummett, Jeremy. *Palermo, City of Kings: The Heart of Sicily*. London ; New York: I.B.Tauris, 2015.

Dunbabin, Jean. *The French in the Kingdom of Sicily, 1266–1305*. Cambridge, UK: Cambridge University Press, 2011.

Edwards, Andrew, and Suzanne Edwards. *Sicily:: A Literary Guide for Travellers*. London: I.B.Tauris, 2014.

"Essay: Lampedusa's 'The Leopard,' Fifty Years on - The New York Times." Accessed April 30, 2019. https://www.nytimes.com/2008/07/29/arts/29iht-booktue.1.14826755.html.

Farrell, Joseph. *Sicily: A Cultural History*. Northampton, MA: Interlink Publishing Group, Incorporated, 2013.

Fentress, James. *Rebels and Mafiosi: Death in a Sicilian Landscape*. Ithaca, NY: Cornell University Press, 2018.

Gambacorta, Giovanni Evangelista di Blasi e. *Storia civile del regno di Sicilia*. Palermo, It: Reale Stamperia, 1818.

Giarrizzo, Giuseppe. *Mezzogiorno senza meridionalismo: la Sicilia, lo sviluppo, il potere*. Venice: Marsilio Editore, 1992.

Goethe, Johann Wolfgang von. *Italian Journey, 1786-1788*. New York: Penguin, 1970.

Gregory, Desmond. *Sicily: The Insecure Base : A History of the British Occupation of Sicily, 1806-1815*. London and Toronto: Fairleigh Dickinson Univ Press, 1988.

Karagoz, Claudia, and Giovanna Summerfield. *Sicily and the Mediterranean: Migration, Exchange, Reinvention*. New York: Palgrave Macmillan, 2015.

Keahey, John. *Seeking Sicily: A Cultural Journey Through Myth and Reality in the Heart of the Mediterranean*. New York: St Martin's Press, 2011.

Lampedusa, Giuseppe Tomasi di. *The Leopard*. New York: Pantheon Books, 1960.

Leighton, Robert. *Sicily Before History: An Archaeological Survey from the Palaeolithic to the Iron Age*. Ithaca, NY: Cornell University Press, 1999.

Lowe, Helen. *Unprotected Females in Sicily, Calabria, and on the Top of Mount Aetna*. London: Routledge, Warnes and Routledge, 1859.

Lupo, Salvatore. *History of the Mafia*. New York: Columbia University Press, 2011.

Mallette, Karla. *The Kingdom of Sicily, 1100-1250: A Literary History*. Philadelphia, PA: University of Pennsylvania Press, 2011.

Marrone, Mariano. *Il regno di Sicilia: dai Normanni agli Aragonesi*. Chieti, IT: Solfanelli Editore, 2014.

Maupassant, Guy de. *Sicily*. New York: Italica Press, 2007.

Mendola, Louis, and Jacqueline Alio. *The Peoples of Sicily: A Multicultural Legacy*. Palermo, It: Trinacria Editions, 2014.

Messina, Maria. *Behind Closed Doors: Her Father's House and Other Stories of Sicily*. New York: The Feminist Press at CUNY, 2007.

Monroe, Will Seymour. *The Spell of Sicily: The Garden of the Mediterranean*. Boston, MA: The Page company, 1909.

Moorehead, Caroline. *Human Cargo: A Journey Among Refugees*. New York: Henry Holt and Company, 2007.

Norwich, John Julius. *Sicily: A Short History, from the Greeks to Cosa Nostra*. London: Hodder & Stoughton, 2015.

———. *Sicily: An Island at the Crossroads of History*. New York: Random House Publishing Group, 2015.

Pfuntner, Laura. *Urbanism and Empire in Roman Sicily*. Austin, TX: University of Texas Press, 2019.

Pirandello, Luigi. *Pirandello's Major Plays*. Evanston, IL: Northwestern University Press, 1991.

Prose, Francine. *Sicilian Odyssey*. National Geographic Books, 2011.

Quasimodo, Salvatore, and Jack Bevan. *Complete Poems*. New York: Schocken Books, 1984.

Rapisarda, Carmine. *British and American Writers in Sicily*. Raleigh, NC: Lulu.com, 2012.

———. *David Herbert Lawrence and Sicily*. Raleigh, NC: Lulu.com, 2012.

Riall, Lucy. *Sicily and the Unification of Italy: Liberal Policy and Local Power, 1859-1866*. Oxford, UK: Oxford University Press Incorporated, 1998.

Robb, Peter. *Midnight In Sicily: On Art, Feed, History, Travel and La Cosa Nostra*. New York: Farrar, Straus and Giroux, 2014.

Romeo, Rosario. *Il Risorgimento in Sicilia*. Rome: Laterza, 1973.

Sammartino, Peter, and William Roberts. *Sicily: An Informal History*. New York: Associated University Presse, 2001.

Sciascia, Leonardo. *To Each His Own*. New York: New York Review of Books, 2000.

Sicily and England. A Sketch of Events in Sicily in 1812 & 1848. Illustrated by Vouchers and State Papers. London: James Ridgway, 1849.

Smith, Denis Mack. *Modern Italy: A Political History*. Ann Arbor, MI: University of Michigan Press, 1997.

Soldier's Guide to Sicily. Printing and Stationery Services, M.E.F., 1943.

Southern Italy and Sicily: With Excursions to Malta, Sardinia, Tunis, and Corfu; Handbook for Travellers. K. Baedeker, 1908.

Stefano, George De. *An Offer We Can't Refuse: The Mafia in the Mind of America*. New York: Faber & Faber/Farrar, Straus, Giroux, 2007.

Ward, Ray. *With the Argylls: A Soldier's Memoir*. Edinburgh, UK: Birlinn, 2014.

Free Books by Charles River Editors

We have brand new titles available for free most days of the week. To see which of our titles are currently free, click on this link.

Discounted Books by Charles River Editors

We have titles at a discount price of just 99 cents everyday. To see which of our titles are currently 99 cents, click on this link.

Printed in Great Britain
by Amazon

38878721R00031